Sprout Up

21 Days of Getting to Your Intended Place

Jossalyn Richardson Wilson

Sprout Up: 21 Days of Getting to Your Intended Place
Copyright © 2014 by Jossalyn Richardson Wilson

All rights reserved. No part of this book may be reproduced, distributed or transmitted in any form or by any means, including photocopying, recording, or other electronic or mechanical methods, without prior written permission from the author.

Scriptures taken from the Holy Bible, New International Version®, NIV®. Copyright © 1973, 1978, 1984, 2011 by Biblica, Inc.™ Used by permission of Zondervan. All rights reserved worldwide.www.zondervan.com The "NIV" and "New International Version" are trademarks registered in the United States Patent and Trademark Office by Biblica, Inc.™

Other Scripture references are from the following sources:

New King James Version®. Copyright © 1982 by Thomas Nelson. Used by permission. All rights reserved.

Cover designed by Lebanon Raingam

Author Photo by Lauren Norkum

Published by Jossalyn's Journey (www.jossalynsjourney.com)

Edited by Rain Publishing (www.rainpublishing.com)

Sprout Up! / Jossalyn Richardson Wilson. -- Softcover Ed.
ISBN 978-0-9909925-0-9

Library of Congress Control Number: 2014921665

With Gratitude

I started writing this book at the end of 2012 and I didn't know it. I didn't write any of the messages within, but I started living the messages I share throughout this book. It didn't/doesn't feel good always, learning lessons, being refined—sprouting up. However, I'm grateful God allowed me to have those experiences, and He allows me to continue living experiences that shape me. Lord, thank you for guiding me in this direction, and thank you for allowing me to share with and encourage your people to live intentionally. I'm honored to be on your team.

To my hubby, Darryl, I owe you a HUGE thank you! You have been on this journey with me—late nights, earlier mornings, all of the "can I read this to you really quickly?" questions. You have endured it all. While sprouting, I know there have been times you've wondered about the direction God was taking us, clinched your teeth because the computer light beamed in your face, and sacrificed without complaint to ensure that my dream didn't remain a seed. Thank you for believing in me. Thank you for believing in my dreams, gifts and talents. Thank you for remaining patient. Thank you for stepping up when I needed you to. Thank you for being strong enough to let me be strong and weak. I love you so much! If this isn't the beginning, we're definitely at a great middle place.

Luke Wilson! You have made all the difference in and to me! Your life motivates me. You are and will remain my reason to work hard. You helped me sprout, and I pray my sprouting encourages you to blossom and become the man God desires. Gosh, I love you! Thank you for letting me love you and for being so lovable.

"Ma" I know you're my most dedicated cheerleader. Thank you for always believing in me, being in my corner and supporting my dreams no matter how big or colorful! You inspire my work ethic, my treatment of and belief in people. I appreciate the example you've set before me. Because of your rearing, I'm able to sprout with confidence because it's been planted and watered in me for so long. Thank you for everything! I hope in some very small way I've made you proud. I love you Momma!

To my little, big brothers: Brandon, RaShad and Marquis thank you for letting me express myself ALWAYS, receiving my words in love and being the best brothers I could have asked for in this lifetime. I appreciate you letting me use your lives in my writings. I often say I have such a diverse family and as a result I learned to love all types of people without prejudice or bias, but I also gained memories and experiences that aided in shaping my knowledge, skill and mindset—thank you for being such incredible brothers—incredible men! I love you!

Grandma, Grandma Jody, and MarQuita, thank you for believing in my dreams and supporting me in everything I do. Your love and support do not go unnoticed. I love you so much and I'm so grateful to have you in my life. Thank you!

Mr. Horace and Mrs. Barbara, affectionately FIL and MIL (Pastor and Minister Horace Wilson, Foster's Grove Baptist Church, Chesnee, SC (www.fostersgrovebaptistchurch.org)), you two are the absolute best! I always feel your love and support and it encourages me more than you'll ever know. Thank you for supporting my dreams and believing in me. Thank you for showing excitement (I don't often tell you this, but I need it). I love you both very much!

Tony, Camille, Bryan, and Bethany thank you for loving me. I feel so at home with you guys and appreciate your belief and encouragement.

Your laughter has motivated me in so many ways. Thank you for treating me like your real sister. I couldn't ask for or create better in-law siblings!

To my current pastors, Pastors Lloyd and Pamela Bustard (World Worship Church in Charlotte, NC (www.worldworshipchurch.net)), thank you for having a vision that encourages us to "Think BIG" about the ideas God has for us. Your intentional teachings have inspired me in so many ways, been fodder while writing and helped me reach a new level in my relationship with Christ. Thank you for your heart for God and His people. You have truly made an impact on my life, and I'm grateful for your love and support.

To my home pastor, Pastor W.I. Jenkins and Minister Danita Jenkins (First Baptist Church of Fairforest, Spartanburg, SC (www.firstbaptistchurchoffairforest.com)), thank you for having a children's ministry that gave me opportunities to strengthen my God-given talents. Under your leadership, I not only learned the seriousness of loving and serving God, but I also learned how to study the word, trust in the Lord and apply His teachings to my life. The woman, wife, mother, and servant I believe I am is due in part to your leadership. Thank you for the opportunities you gave me to teach Sunday School, sing on the choir, read the announcements, perform in plays, speak to the youth, the congregation, help plan events, etc. I'm a better woman because you and those in our church family helped train me in the way I should go!

To my mentors: Stacey Joseph Harris (www.staceyjoseph.com), Almeader Howard, and Alphaeus Anderson (www.gainmaintain.com) thank you for agreeing to EVERY request, spending time with me and sharing your wisdom, guidance and expertise—you are truly an inspiration and blessing to my life. I pray God's richest blessings upon you and your ministry. There really aren't words to express my appreciation and deep love for you. Thank you with all of my heart!

I'd like to extend a big thanks to some other VERY important people in my life who listen to me, push me, inspire me, believe in and support me: Mrs. Altie Anderson (my queen), Marcel Anderson (www.marcelanderson.com), Alexius Anderson, Marcus Anderson (www.marcusanderson.net), Ursula Anderson, Brenna Campbell, Monica Graves, Ashley Glenn Robinson, Monica Wade, Sherrian Ellis, Gerik and Kesha Todd, Rocky and Lauren Norkum, Billy and Vinese Cates, Shannon Coleman, Gregory and Danielle Embry, Jerry and Corchanda Means, Mrs. Barbara Jones, Mr. Maceo and Mrs. Dorothy Black, D. LeVar and Katie Moore, Alan Young, Joslyn Gaines, Reggie and Crystal Wright, Deirdre Maxwell, Maceo Harris, Cedric Miller, Mrs. Willa Reeder, Flossie Hughes, every single person who subscribes to and reads my blog Jotting Truth (www.jottingtruth.com), the entire First Baptist Church of Fairforest, Foster's Grove Baptist Church and World Worship Church, Melissa DeLoach, Mrs. Fran Price, all of my aunts, uncles and cousins—thank you, thank you, thank you. If I failed to name you in this book don't worry, more are coming, God's will. ☺

With humble gratitude,
Jossalyn

In Loving Memory

Aaron Anderson
Minnie Hines "Granny"
Ayden James
Leonard Richardson "Pan-Pa"
Catherine Taylor

Thank you for everything, seen and unseen.

CONTENTS

Before you Begin...
My Story...1
There's a Choice to Make...3
Pen not Pencil 5
Dig Up the Roots...7
A Lap Today, Two Laps Tomorrow..11
Only Trash Goes in the Trashcan..15
Unicorns and Fairy Princesses… It's all Make Believe......................19
Learning a New Language...23
Seek Counsel...25
Submit!..29
Completion 31
The Pill to Swallow 35
Become Weary or Reap 37
Spending & Investing 39
Faithful to the Few..43
Not Some Things..47
The –Ing Family 51
Double Vanities: Thanking...53
Praise the Lord: Celebrating 55
Different Kinds: Resting 59
Give like Jesus: Giving 63
Be Strategic: Praying 67
It's More than Important: Fasting...73
As you Grow…...77

Before you begin...

One vice I have is expecting from others what I expect of myself—I wouldn't ask you to do something I am not willing to do. My husband argues that I can't place the same pressure on someone else that I place on myself because "everyone is different." While I agree to an extent, I believe something special happens when you make a sacrifice and commit yourself to a cause, a purpose, a mission.

I'm asking that you do dig deep and challenge yourself to remain committed, give God everything you have and watch Him transform your life. I'm asking you to give God 21 days, and no matter what you face or witness, don't look back.

I've lived what I've shared throughout this book. I've had to learn how to live a balanced life, holding both my passions and responsibilities in the same hand, and sometimes I failed miserably. I'm guilty of procrastinating (I could probably earn a gold medal in this field), getting weary when I don't hear God (which always feels like the time I'm longing to hear Him the most), trying to make things happen in my own strength, questioning how resources would come, or stopping midstream because I've gotten distracted. I've second and third guessed myself and gotten so consumed with the details they paralyzed me.

Yet with all of those human emotions, I could still feel something brewing inside me—my kingdom purpose. Something growing and taking form all on its own, something so deep it had to come out.
So yes, I'm asking you to purpose in your heart that you will move forward and put in the work to fulfill God's plan for your life. I pray

my sprout encourages, challenges and inspires your seed to take root and come forth. Sprout now! Sprout Up!

My Story

"There came a time when the risk to remain tight in the bud was more painful than the risk it took to blossom." Anais Nin

I quit my job because I wanted to sprout. I knew I didn't want my 50 year-old self to look at my 30 year-old self and question, "What were you afraid of?" And, for what felt like the first time in my life, I wasn't making a decision that made sense to other people or even complete sense to me, but I knew I had to jump if I were ever going to get to the place God intended.

For me, it was the fear of leaving a position where I worked 50+ hours every week, created materials that often seemed overlooked, spent countless hours rehashing details that I'm still not sure would have led to the outcome we were promoting and seeing results that were NEVER indicative of all the work, thought, emotion, care, or attention gone into "them." Yet, when it all came down to it, I felt like God actually put His hand on my back and pushed me to make me leave. Why would I keep holding on, fighting, and insisting when God was saying, "Go!" "Jump!" "Sprout up!"

Staying in the bud got painful.

I'm sure you'd like me to tell you I left and didn't look back. Well, it did happen that way for the most part, but looking back actually helped me see what I'd learned and why I had to have that experience.

God has called you to a purpose, but sometimes getting there seems like an obstacle course of unending jumps, turns, races, and falls. Before you know it, all the energy you started off with is depleted by the vigor of the race and bruised knees. God has an intended place for you, but first you must be willing to grow!

If living within the bud hasn't become painful, I'm sorry to say, but I doubt that you're ready to get to the place God has for you. But, if it's feeling awfully tight where you are, and you keep feeling like there is something inside you getting ready to burst—it's time to sprout up.

The world is waiting and ready for you to blossom.

There's a Choice to Make

Today's Truth: "Simply let your 'Yes' be 'Yes' and your 'No,' 'No;' anything beyond this comes from the evil one." ~ Matthew 5:37 NIV

There's a Choice to Make

Before you're able to grow you will have to embrace what was likely one of your first words: No.

Go ahead, open your mouth and say it, "No!"

"No" is important because it actually helps you determine three things:
1. What matters to you
2. What can and has to wait (and)
3. What will not get your attention

It's also important to recognize that "no" looks differently for different people.

I had to say "no" to 50+ hour weeks and feeling my talents and contributions were overlooked, undervalued, and continuously questioned and critiqued. I also had to say "no" to the idea that I was quitting.

You could be saying "no" to being torn down, "no" to living paycheck to paycheck, or "no" to the opportunity that seemingly makes the most sense to everyone around you.

The risk associated with "no" often holds us back. For example, if you're saying "no" to a job, the risk could be not having enough money for your household. Or, it could mean not having a routine etched out for you, or not being sure how to spend your time.

Jesus teaches us that our "yes" should be "yes" and our "no," "no;" anything else is confusion—not of God.

In 1 Kings 18:21, Elijah asked the people, "How long will you waver between two opinions?"

There's a choice to make! Determine what you will say "no" to today. Stick to your decision, and be confident in God's leading.

In Application

Which areas of your life need a "no?" And, by saying "no," which area(s) are getting a "yes?" Journal your responses.

Prayer

Heavenly Father, thank you for the gift of choice. Give me the fortitude to remain committed to my "yes" and "no." Grant me wisdom to determine the answer needed for every area of my life and give me the strength to stick to it. Your word teaches that a double-minded man is unstable in all of his ways (James 1:8). I will be stable; I am stable in Jesus' name, Amen.

Pen not Pencil

Today's Truth: "Write down the revelation and make it plain on tablets so that anyone who sees it may run with it. For the revelation awaits an appointed time; it speaks of the end and will not prove false. Though it linger, wait for it; it will certainly come and will not delay."
~Habakkuk 2:2-3 NIV

Pen not Pencil

There's something about a pen that's permanent.

When signing a contract for a house, a car title, or marriage license, you'd never write those in pencil because it's too easy to wiggle out of the agreement. Putting your signature in pen indicates commitment, and it sends the message that no matter what, I'm sticking with and to "it."

To successfully sprout, you'll need to make a commitment, binding yourself to your purpose. Recording your vision is essential to your growth because it holds you accountable when other ideas, situations, or circumstances pop up and seemingly beg you to disregard the goals you've established.

Habakkuk 2:2-3 reads, "Write down the revelation and make it plain on tablets so that anyone who sees it may run with it. For the revelation awaits an appointed time; it speaks of the end and will not prove false. Though it linger, wait for it; it will certainly come and will not delay."

Record your plan! It's the first step to seeing your vision become reality. Writing your vision holds you accountable to completing the task you started.

Get excited, you are beginning your predestined journey—God is pleased!

In Application

Grab a notebook and pen, and record your vision!

Prayer

Heavenly Father, show me the place you intend for me. Forgive me for neglecting your vision. Show me what you desire for my life and I will record and stick with the vision you share. No longer will I delay in the plans you have for me. I'm starting today by putting pen to paper and writing the vision you have for my life, in Jesus' name I pray, Amen.

Dig Up the Roots

Today's Truth: "This year you will eat what grows by itself, and the second year what springs from that. But in the third year sow and reap, plant vineyards and eat their fruit." ~2 Kings 19:29 NIV

Dig Up the Roots

Social innovationists go through a process before actualizing their idea. They spend countless hours researching and analyzing the symptoms that exist from the problem they are aiming to solve to ensure they are attacking root causes.

Specifically, they know a problem exists and name the top three symptoms occurring as a result. From there, they ask themselves, 'Why?' at minimum, three times per symptom. These entrepreneurs understand that if change is truly going to occur and last, they must attack the root.

It's great to establish goals and make yourself promises, but true and lasting change will not exist if you don't attack the root. Oftentimes we don't attack the root because it's easier to deal with the symptoms. Symptoms don't go as deep as roots, nor do symptoms have the strength of roots.

Getting to the root requires work. It takes **self**-reflection and commitment. But, once you reach the root and plant new seeds, you and those connected to you will appreciate your work and results. When you determine the symptoms of your life, you can attack the root. Pushing yourself to ask and answer your "why" may present a challenge and force true reflection, but it is worth it.

In the nineteenth chapter of 2 Kings, the Assyrians understood what they were going to reap generated from the root and the remnants of their fruit would continue to produce as well.

What roots do you need to deal with in order to understand the fruit you are seeing in your life? Don't allow another year, month or day to go by dealing with weeds. Stop procrastinating! Dig up the roots, plant vineyards and eat the fruit God intends for you.

In Application

Perform a Root Exposure Assessment to dig up the areas of your life that require change.

Prayer

Dear Lord, thank you for saying "whatsoever a man sows that shall he reap." I will take time to get to the root of the things and/or people that are holding me back, and I'll take time to understand how to attack the roots that aren't yielding the fruit you or I desire in my life. Give me the strength to get clear and honest with myself because I trust your word, and I know your principles will work in my life, in Jesus' name, Amen.

Root Exposure Assessment

The Root Exposure Assessment (REA) requires you to dig deep to uncover what is keeping you from your purpose. Be honest with yourself; expose the root so you can experience the change you are seeking.

Root Exposure Assessment (Example)	
Self-Awareness:	I realize I am not committed to finishing a task that requires multiple steps.
Symptom:	I don't finish things I set out to accomplish.
Ask yourself... Why:	I don't finish things because I do not understand how to manage my time effectively.
Ask again...Why:	I do not understand how to manage my time effectively because I feel like I need to complete things in sequential order or I don't allot enough time to each task.
And again...Why:	I enjoy freedom and fear that managing time will mean eliminating activities I do for pleasure and will hold me accountable.
Root Cause:	I struggle with commitment because I know it will shift how I spend my time and make me accountable, and I fear change. I don't want to change because I do not want to explore new feelings.

Root Exposure Assessment	
Self-Awareness	
Symptom:	
Ask yourself... Why:	
Ask again...Why:	
And again...Why:	
Root Cause:	

A Lap Today, Two Laps Tomorrow

Today's Truth: "Suppose one of you wants to build a tower. Will he not first sit down and estimate the cost to see if he has enough money to complete it? For if he lays the foundation and is not able to finish it, everyone who sees it will ridicule him, saying, 'This fellow began to build and was not able to finish.'" ~Luke 14: 28-30 NIV

A Lap Today, Two Laps Tomorrow

I'm sure you've heard the saying, "failing to plan is planning to fail." There have been times when I've bitten off more than I could chew, times where I didn't have a solid plan. I had a vision, but I hadn't taken time to map out the details, the building blocks in order to achieve my vision.

As a visionary, it can be difficult sometimes to focus on the nuances that ensure you reach your goals, but it's necessary. Jesus told the disciples, "Following me will cost," meaning, you'll have to be willing to give something up to gain something you've never had. When you're giving something up to attain something new, you need a plan. When I left my job I gave something up to follow God's purpose for my life, but pursuing my purpose required a plan.

The vision God has trusted you with will cost. It will cost monetarily, through your time and energy, and it will require you to have a plan with concrete, measurable goals. Your plan will help you determine how much time, money, and energy it will take to ensure that you don't start something you're not able to finish.

I have runner-friends; some who have run in competitions for titles. They envision themselves smiling, sprinting across the finish-line in victory, but they also realize all the work it requires, time it will take, and training they'll have to pursue to win the race, or compete on a high level. They count up the cost.

Maybe this is the first time you've stepped out to pursue something of this magnitude, and you know what you want to see accomplished by the end. Take the time to think about all the steps it will require to get to your anticipated place.

You want to see your vision become reality? Count up the cost and establish your goals. A plan is vital to your success.

In Application

Using the Sprout Up Goal Sheet, generate concrete and measureable goals that will help you reach your vision. Your goal sheet becomes your "to-do" list.

Prayer

Heavenly Father, thank you for pushing me to count up the cost in following and pursuing the plan you have for my life. Allow me to remain diligent so I may accomplish the goals before me. Thank you for clear thoughts and direction. I will determine the actionable, bite-sized steps it will take for me to fulfill the vision you've placed in my heart, in Jesus' name, Amen.

Sprout Up Goal Sheet

Goal: *What do I want to accomplish?*	
Knowledge (K), Skill (S), and Mindset (M): *What will I need to learn, do, and/or believe in order to accomplish my goal?*	
Time: *How much time do I want to spend on this goal (i.e. weeks, months)?*	
Actions to take during allotted timeframe:	
Measure of Success: *What will it look like when I accomplish my goal?*	

Sprout Up Goal Sheet

Goal: *What do I want to accomplish?*	
Knowledge (K), Skill (S), and Mindset (M): *What will I need to learn, do, and/or believe in order to accomplish my goal?*	
Time: *How much time do I want to spend on this goal (i.e. weeks, months)?*	
Actions to take during allotted timeframe:	
Measure of Success: *What will it look like when I accomplish my goal?*	

Only Trash Goes in the Trashcan

Today's Truth: "So do not throw away your confidence; it will be richly rewarded. You need to persevere so that when you have done the will of God, you will receive what He has promised." ~Hebrews 10:35-36 NIV

Only Trash Goes in the Trashcan

How many things do you throw away every day? Really take a second to think about it. Between work, home, and errands, I'm sure you visit a trashcan quite often and sometimes unconsciously.

We dispose of so many things that we sometimes get rid of the wrong things, and before we know it our hopes, dreams, and confidence are tossed out with yesterday's garbage.

Your confidence is thrown away when you stop believing in the gifts and talents God has given you. Your confidence is thrown away when you neglect to believe that God has an ordained purpose and plan for your life, you stop working towards the plan and vision He placed in your heart, or you allow others to mishandle your confidence through their words or deeds.

I'm sure there's a trashcan in almost every room in your home, but those bins aren't for your confidence.

If you've thrown your confidence away, it's not too late to get it back.

Start by determining where you left it. Going back to that place in thought will help you uncover what happened that caused you to doubt yourself. Maybe it was the constant let down from someone you love and trust, or maybe you're feeling like you failed once and you'll fail again. No matter what, snatch your confidence out of the trashcan and begin to clean it off. You will need your confidence as you sprout up.

In Application

Journal about the incident(s) that caused you to throw your confidence away. Using the Confidence Keeper note, determine one thing that will boost and keep your confidence. Jot what keeps your confidence in a place you frequent (examples: a note in the car, in your bathroom, closet door, or on your desk).

Prayer

> *Heavenly Father, I threw my confidence away when (name the time and or place you lost your confidence). Give me the fortitude to face that situation and take my confidence back. I know that it is Satan's job to kill, steal, and destroy, but I will not allow him to kill, steal, or destroy my confidence. I know the passion you placed in my heart will come to pass. I believe in myself and I believe in you, in Jesus' name, Amen.*

Confidence Keeper

○

○

○

Unicorns and Fairy Princesses... It's all Make Believe

Today's Truth: "Do you not know? Have you not heard? The Lord is the everlasting God, the Creator of the ends of the earth. He will not grow tired or weary, and His understanding no one can fathom. He gives strength to the weary and increases the power of the weak." ~Isaiah 40:28-29 NIV

Unicorns and Fairy Princesses...It's all Make Believe

Somewhere along the way you stopped believing in the Tooth Fairy and Santa Claus, likely due to something someone told you.

Perchance it was your mother who sat with you and shared she was actually the person slipping those dollar and five dollar bills under your pillow when you lost a tooth. Or, maybe your father confessed he ate the cookies and drank the milk you left for Santa Claus on Christmas Eve. No matter how it happened, you eventually reached a certain age or level of maturity and you stopped believing.

We often run into this same problem in our lives. We start out believing God with all our might, but as life happens and we face more challenges and experiences, we stop believing God. No, you don't stop believing in God, but you stop believing He's capable of opening doors, coming through, or making ways that are seemingly impossible. We stop believing He can bless us this week because He did it last week, and two times in a row seems unreal. We marginalize God's strength, majesty, and power to human nature, and we begin seeing His abilities through our limited view.

God has a purpose for you, one that He placed inside you as He knit you together in your mother's womb. Don't stop believing in His ability to get you to your intended place. Yes, life will throw curveballs, but God catches those and throws the ball back in your favor for a homerun.

God is everlasting. He does not grow weary or tired. The vision He placed in your heart is not a figment of your imagination. It's not make-believe or pretend. Your purpose is God-breathed and inspired. Don't stop believing.

Don't give up on your dreams because things aren't going as quickly as you'd like or even the way you desire—God is getting you there!

In Application

Journal one area you will submit to God and specifically name how you will demonstrate your trust in Him.

Prayer

Heavenly Father, thank you for being real, alive, and everlasting. Thank you for being able to handle my fears and desires, and never growing weary or tired and reminding me that I have the power to tread over serpents. Lord, there have been occurrences that have caused me to question if you would come through, and I've wondered if you were still listening and concerned with the desires of my heart. Forgive me for doubting you, your word and your promises to me. I will not equate your majestic power to human abilities. I will be confident in you and trust you with everything, in Jesus' name I pray, Amen.

Learning a New Language

Today's Truth: "Let no corrupting talk come out of your mouths, but only such as is good for building up, as fits the occasion, that it may give grace to those who hear." ~Ephesians 4:29 ESV

Learning a New Language

As a high school and college prerequisite, you're likely asked to take a foreign language. In that course, you often learn the dialect, vernacular and even some of the customs associated with the native speakers.

As you grow in comfort with the language, you tend to embrace usage a bit more, picking up on negative words, colloquialisms and portions of the jargon. Before you know it, you're speaking your new language with less thought.

The same happens with your native tongue. As you learned new words and gained more confidence in speaking, there's often less intentionality and thought when forming sentences or pronouncing new words.

Losing intentionality when we speak often causes us to speak damaging prophesies over our future and lives. The bible teaches, "The tongue has the power of life and death, and those who love it will eat its fruit" (Proverbs 18:21).

If your speech has become lackadaisical you are likely destroying your future, your vision, and your dreams with your words. Oftentimes we take our words for granted and we speak without thought, using language that leaves a damaging residue. Talk is **not** cheap! You'll pay a big price for speaking negatively.

Are you speaking negatively because you've experienced failure or setbacks? Has a sickness caused you to stop speaking life? Don't dig graves with your words. Your words should build up and extend grace to others. Stop speaking without thought and get intentional about affirming your future and your life.

Your season of sprouting is new, speak intentionally!

In Application

Language has the power to shape your vision, both the way you see and embrace it. Create five one-two sentence affirmations that you will speak over your life, vision, and future. Your affirmations will help you remain on track towards accomplishing your goals.

Prayer

> *O Lord, set a guard over my mouth and keep a watch over the door of my lips. Fill my mouth with blessings. Help me become intentional about the things I speak over my future. Forgive me for becoming so comfortable with my words that I neglected to speak positive affirmations. I will speak intentionally. I declare, "The plans of the Lord stand firm forever;" therefore I will not doubt (Psalm 33:11). I speak "no eye has seen, no ear has heard, no mind has conceived" what you have prepared for me (1 Corinthians 2:9-10). Thank you for giving me the language to use to yield fruit in my life. My future is bright because of you; in Jesus' name, Amen.*

Seek Counsel

Today's Truth: "Plans fail for lack of counsel, but with many advisers they succeed." ~Proverbs 15:22 NIV

Seek Counsel

Deciding to get married is one of the biggest decisions I've made thus far. Full of young excitement and fresh love, I knew Darryl and I were meant to live the rest of our lives together in marital bliss. But even with all of the certainty and assurance in our forever, we knew we needed to seek counsel if we were going to have a true shot at living together in holy matrimony. So, we took premarital counseling and even have check-ups throughout our marriage because we recognize we are two imperfect people attempting to live the rest of our lives together as one.

While we have an incredible marriage, we know those who have experienced marriage longer have valuable insight and wisdom to offer. Maybe they offer tips on arguing fairly, how to handle in-laws, having children, intimacy, what not to do, how to have difficult conversations, or understanding how to manage money; we value their experiences and appreciate them freely sharing their hearts. However, Darryl and I didn't just choose 'any-ol'-body' to give us advice; we sought counsel from our pastors and those who conduct their marriage according to God's design.

As you make plans to actualize your God-given vision, seek counsel. Use wisdom when determining who to ask for advice. It wouldn't make much sense to ask a single person, who has never experienced marriage how to live together as one for forty-plus years.

When seeking counsel, use wisdom. Pray and consult God on the people you are considering sharing your ideas and dreams with; this is your future, your vision, your life—choose wisely and seek counsel.

In Application

Generate a list of attributes you need and want in those you consult about your plans. Determine who fits the description, prepare your questions, and then ask them for help. You can use the Mentor Ask if you want or need guidance in asking a person for help.

Prayer

> *Heavenly Father, thank you for connecting me with people who have the knowledge, skill, and wisdom to share with me as I work towards actualizing the vision you've placed in my heart. Forgive me for having the mindset that I don't need others and I'm able to handle everything on my own. I will use wisdom and seek counsel because I realize the vision you have given me is bigger than me. Thank you for sending the right mentors my way. I will not mishandle them or their time. I will drop my self-righteous attitude, ask for help, be prepared, and apply the knowledge I gain, in Jesus' name I pray, Amen.*

Mentor Ask

Example 1
Hello _____,

I hope you are well today. I would like you to know how much I admire your ability to _____. I have watched you practice this skill for many years and learned so much from your wisdom and expertise. As I pursue the path God has for me in _____, I know I will need guidance along the way. Having watched, learned from, and admired your leadership from afar, I would like to ask for your personal guidance regarding my passion(s).

If you have 30 minutes to share your knowledge with me, I would appreciate your counsel.

Thank you for setting an excellent example.

I'm honored to know you,

Your Name

Example 2 (If you have taken steps towards your vision)
Hello _____,

I hope you are well today. I would like you to know how much I admire your ability to _____. I have watched you practice this skill for many years and learned so much from your wisdom and expertise. As I pursue the path God has for me in _____, I know I will need guidance along the way. Having watched, learned from, and admired your leadership from afar I would like to ask for your personal guidance regarding my passion(s).

Most recently, I have (insert precise steps you have taken towards learning more or building skill as it relates to actualizing your vision. Example: I've read _____, conducted research on _____, spoken with _____, and held a focus group with _____).

While I've gained valuable information, I know there is more to learn. If you have 30 minutes to share your knowledge with me, I would appreciate your counsel.

Thank you for setting an excellent example.

I'm honored to know you,

Your Name

Submit!

Today's Truth: "What you ought to say is, 'If the Lord wants us to, we shall live and do this or that.' Otherwise you will be bragging about your own plans, and such self-confidence never pleases God." ~James 4:15-16 TLB

Submit!

I don't brag about things I'm able to do, but there is a bit of personal satisfaction in knowing I can do something. I don't believe God is off-put or offended when we have confidence. In fact, He wants us to have confidence; He does however want our confidence streamed through Him.

As you acquire more knowledge and build more skill, your confidence in your abilities and talents increases. However, we should not become so confident in ourselves that we forget that God is in control of everything. On the path to becoming what God has called you, you will likely increase in recognition, name, and even economic standing, but do not allow your increase to cause you to forget how weak you are without Christ.

Our plans and decisions should be committed to God's agenda, meaning, everything you do and desire should have God at the forefront. Don't let your plans cloud your vision. Don't become overly confident in yourself. Don't forget that the work of your hands comes from the Lord. Submit your plans to Him to ensure that what you are doing is what He wants, and how you're behaving and treating others is pleasing to Him.

In Application

Ensure your goals are submissive to God by reading the fourth chapter in the book of James (which teaches you how to submit to God), and journal your thoughts. Then, give God all the credit for where you are in life and what you are obtaining.

Prayer

> *Heavenly Father, I submit my goals, desires, and plans to you. I will not forget that my life is like a mist that appears for a little while and then vanishes. Therefore, I will not become so confident in myself that I fail to recognize your power at work in my life. Thank you for every blessing you have given me, and thank you for trusting me with your provision, in Jesus' name I pray, Amen.*

Completion

Today's Truth: "I am confident of the very thing, that He who began a good work in you will carry it on to completion until the day of Christ Jesus." ~ Philippians 1:6 NASB

Completion

In grade school, if you asked any of my teachers, I'm sure they'd tell you I was typically one of the last students to complete an assignment or test. Although I studied and prepared for the test or assignment it seemed to always take me a little longer to finish for some reason. What my teachers couldn't tell you is that it slightly bothered me that I seemed to always finish last.

In my mind I felt finishing close to the end or at the end meant others understood more or were smarter, or that people were forming opinions about my working style, my intelligence, or even questioning my abilities. Finishing close to the end or at the end, made me feel bad because it meant that other people were waiting on me.

Sometimes it can feel like you are finishing last or it is taking you longer than others to reach your destiny. You work hard, you treat people fairly, and you really try to do the right things, but it still feels like you're coming in last.

Friend, take courage in knowing that God has begun a good work in you, and He will not stop shaping and molding you into the likeness of His son until His return. The work God has called your hands to perform will be complete. Don't allow Satan to place a trap in your mind causing you to think or believe others are getting there or further along. When you realize you are uniquely created, you understand you aren't in competition with anyone. You are right where God wants you. Our God delivers and prevails; He will not stop what He's started.

Trust God in this process. It may feel like it's taking a bit longer to reach your destiny, but it's worth it. Maybe He's increasing your faith, refining your skill, allowing experiences to build your audience—no matter what, He'll finish what He started.

In Application

Allow God to complete the work He's started in you by submitting to His authority in your mind and body. Submit to God in your mind and body by reciting the Sprout Up Truths to indicate your trust in God's ability to finish the work He's started in you.

Prayer

> *Lord, I confess I am a sinner, but I openly profess that Jesus died and was resurrected for my sinful nature and now He is seated at your right hand. God, if you could complete the work you started in Jesus, I know you can complete the work you've started in me. I'll stop being insecure in my abilities, talent and intellect and see myself as your work, pliable to your liking. Complete me, in Jesus' name, Amen.*

Sprout Up Truths

"God does not desire for my wait to become weight; therefore, I will be anxious for nothing." ~Philippians 4:6

"God will complete the work He's started in me; for that reason, I am prosperous, I have hope, and a future." ~Jeremiah 29:11

"In you Lord God, I put my trust; I know you will guide my plans." ~Psalm 25:1

The Pill to Swallow

Today's Truth: "I am not saying this because I am in need, for I have learned to be content whatever the circumstance. I know what it is to be in need, and I know what it is to have plenty. I have learned the secret of being content in any and every situation, whether well fed or hungry, whether living in plenty or in want. I can do everything through Him who gives me strength." ~Philippians 4:11-13 NIV

The Pill to Swallow

Our human nature says we deserve. I work hard, I deserve to drive a nice car, carry nice handbags, and live in a nice house. I graduated from college; I deserve to be able to find a job with a great salary and benefits. I give; I deserve to receive. I pray; I deserve to get answers. We put stipulations on what we do and what we believe is owed to us.

News Flash!

God doesn't owe you anything. You have not earned the future you are trying to reach, God doesn't owe it to you and there's really nothing you can do to deserve it. What you truly deserve, God didn't allow—death, hell, and the grave.

Don't become fixated on where you are going, or trying so desperately to get there because you think it's the life you deserve. Don't miss the opportunity to enjoy contentment right where you are. Paul said it best in Philippians, "Whatever the circumstance, I've learned to be content because no matter what circumstance I face, it's Christ's strength that allows me to be in that state."

With only 13 dollars in the bank until Friday, it's Christ's strength that keeps me. I can't find a job and my bills are piling up, yet I can do all things through Christ who gives me strength. Maybe tonight is filet mignon at a five star restaurant, I don't deserve it; it's Christ's strength that allows me this experience.

When you take the valley personal, you will take the mountaintop personal too. I know it's a pill to swallow to think about all the things you've done and know those acts won't get you what you want or where you want. God doesn't owe you anything. Once you swallow that pill, humility kicks in and your heart becomes grateful. Thank God for your current state.

In Application

Accept that your good still doesn't deserve God's glory. Create a Gratitude List, listing reasons you are grateful.

Prayer

Heavenly Father, I don't deserve your love or any of the blessings you grant. Thank you for your strength that keeps me no matter the state or condition. I recognize that my "righteous acts are as filthy rags" (Isaiah 64:6). I repent for acting like I deserve your blessings, your love, you keeping me—God I don't deserve any of it. I will be content whether abased or abound because I know you are with me in the valley and on the mountaintop. Thank you for being faithful, in Jesus' name. Amen.

Become Weary or Reap

Today's Truth: "Let us not become weary in doing good, for at the proper time we will reap a harvest if we do not give up." ~Galatians 6:9 NIV

Become Weary or Reap

The word weary, is often defined as being exhausted in strength, endurance, vigor or freshness. Paul reminds us that we should not become weary in doing what's right, meaning, we can't grow tired of the things of God. We can't stop being kind, generous, loving, patient, or self-controlled. If we do, we sacrifice our harvest.

Sacrificing the harvest should not be an option for you. You have worked diligently doing the things God has called you to do, and the harvest has promised to afford abundance—more than what you have right now.

We can become weary. If the possibility of weariness were not true, Paul would not have suggested that we should not become weary in doing good. We get tired of doing the right things at times because the harvest doesn't present itself immediately. Whether we admit it or not, we all want a bit of incentive from time to time.

There will be and are days that you feel like nothing is going right, days in which you are tired in strength, endurance, vigor, and freshness; however, you cannot become weary.

Your harvest is shifting beneath the ground. Seeds that you've planted are bursting forth. Buds are forming in your favor. Your harvest is sprouting up. Don't get tired. Don't give up. Don't stop planting the things you desire to reap. You will receive your harvest if you choose not to become weary.

In Application

Keep going! Find at least one way to sow a seed in favor of your harvest.

Prayer

Dear Lord, give me the strength to not grow weary in well-doing. Lord, I confess that sometimes it's hard to keep going, and I want to stop. But, I know you have promised me a harvest if I do not faint. Therefore, I will keep going and obey your commands. When I become tired, renew my mind, my body and my belief. Thank you for teaching me how to be a faithful planter. I will appreciate my harvest so much more because I understand the faithfulness that goes into sowing, the attention it requires to tend to my seeds and the patience exerted in waiting. I'm excited about my harvest, in Jesus' name, Amen.

Spending & Investing

Today's Truth: "Do not store up for yourselves treasures on earth, where moths and vermin destroy, and where thieves break in and steal. But store up for yourselves treasure in heaven, where moths and vermin do not destroy, and where thieves do not break in and steal. For where your treasure is, there your heart will be also." ~Matthew 6:19-21 NIV

Spending & Investing

Ever heard the phrase, "That money is going to burn a hole in your pocket?" As children, the minute we were given money for a birthday, a pulled tooth, or an allowance, we were ready to spend. However, there were those few occasions in which we wanted something more than the money we had could afford, so we had to save what we'd been given or earned in order to make the bigger purchase.

Well, this time, I wanted to save my money so I could open a checking and savings account. I was able to get the accounts in high school (one of those adult-shared accounts) when I started working.

The minute I had the accounts, I wanted to learn how to invest my money in stocks. I knew that if I intentionally didn't spend my money and invested in a solid stock, I would make more money than the original cost of the stock—getting more out than I put in initially.

In Matthew 6:19-21, Jesus is telling us to be intentional about our investments. When we funnel our time, energy, money, feelings, efforts, and thoughts into things of this world, our treasures are susceptible to the destruction of moths and other pests. We will NOT have a return on what we put in.

When we are intentional, and we invest time ministering God's word to a discouraged person, we invest our money into the work of the Lord, or we invest our talents and gifts to edify and bring glory to God, we are storing up treasures in heaven.

Think about occasions you've invested time with a person and then you watch them grow in God's calling for their life. For the times you invested your talents and gifts to help others, there is a reward.

Spending is different than investing. When we spend, there isn't a return. When we invest, we yield more than we put in. The word tells us to "store up…treasure in heaven," meaning, invest in your heavenly stock! Spending depletes, investing multiplies! Invest!

In Application

Be intentional! Invest in your heavenly treasures. "For where your treasure is, there your heart will be also" (Matthew 6:21). What can you invest today? Make a decision and start sowing!

Prayer

Dear Lord, thank you for your wisdom. Thank you for telling me where to store my treasure in order to see the best reward. Help me not to lose focus on how and where to invest. Today, I will invest in my heavenly treasures, knowing that you will increase my harvest if I do not faint. I love you, and I pray this prayer in Jesus' name, Amen.

Faithful to the Few

Today's Truth: "He who is faithful in what is least, is faithful also in much; and he who is unjust in what is least is unjust also in much." ~Luke 16:10 KJV

Faithful to the Few

I had a student once who didn't have everything she needed for school. She didn't have pencils, notebooks, markers, or even a backpack to begin the school year. Can you imagine showing up for work and not having something you needed?

However, this young lady was by far one of my best students. When she arrived she worked diligently and put forth her best effort. Her grades were stellar and her attitude was incomparable. Today, this young lady who showed up to my class with very little on the outside has received a scholarship to college, and she is only a freshman in high school.

Will you be faithful over what you have?

Maybe you only have the first page of your book complete—remain faithful.

The job you have may pay very little and not give you the respect you deserve—remain faithful.

The car you drive may not be top-of-the-line—remain faithful.

At home, you may be experiencing relationships that are in disarray and developing your patience—remain faithful.

You are suffering financially, don't stop giving—remain faithful.

You see, my student who showed up with very little, remained faithful, and she was rewarded. Her reward came *before* society would have expected and even *before* the need existed.

God wants to see your faithfulness right where you are. And, when He sees that you can be faithful in what is least, He knows you will be faithful in abundance. No matter where you are right now and how little you feel you have, show God your faithfulness. Do not despise small beginnings (Zechariah 4:10).

He will reward your faithfulness!

In Application

God wants to see your faithfulness right where you are. Exhibit faithfulness in everything you have; God will multiply in His timing. Use the Measure Your Faithfulness survey to see where your gratitude shows up most.

Prayer

> *Dear Lord, thank you for teaching me faithfulness with little. Because of this place God, I will have a deeper appreciation for the place you desire to take me. God, please continue to show yourself faithful in my life so I may experience all that you have for me. I will remain faithful right where I am, and I trust that you will reward my faithfulness. I love you and I pray this prayer in Jesus' name, Amen.*

Measure Your Faithfulness

1. Are you dedicated to the tasks God gives you?
   - All the time (75%-100%)
   - Most of the time (50%-75%)
   - Rarely (25%-50%)
   - Not at all (0-25%)

2. How do you demonstrate your faithfulness to the tasks God has given you? List at least 2 ways.
   a.

   b.

3. Are you developing your God-given gifts and talents? Consider 1 Peter 4:10.

   _____

4. How are you developing your God-given gifts and talents? List at least 2 ways.
   a.

   b.

5. Do you keep your word? Consider Proverbs 20:25.

   _____

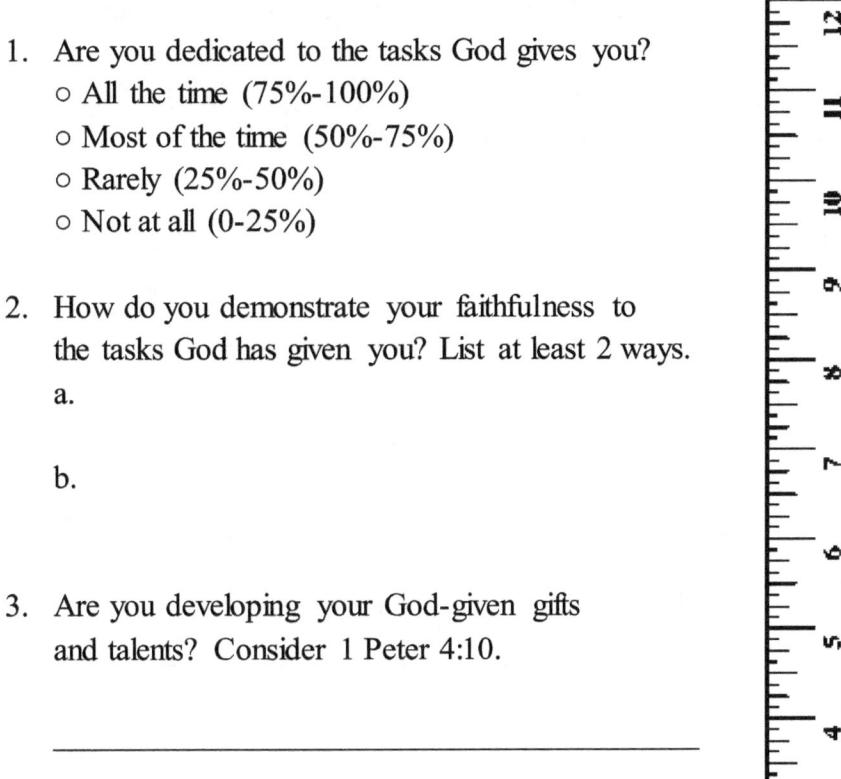

6. What measures can you take to keep your word more often? (Examples: using wisdom by scheduling less events, planning for more time on projects, spending more time understanding how faithful God is to you, etc.) List at least 2 ways.
   a.

   b.

7. Are you concerned about others? Consider Proverbs 28:20.

   _____

8. How can you show concern for others?

   _____
   _____
   _____

9. How does God show faithfulness to you? Consider Psalm 23:1-6, Psalm 85: 1-6, 2 Timothy 2:13, 1 Corinthians 10:13, 2 Thessalonians 3:3, Hebrew 11:6.

   _____
   _____

Not <u>Some</u> Things

Today's Truth: "In everything give thanks; for this is the will of God in Christ Jesus for you." ~1 Thessalonians 5:18 NKJV

Not SOME Things

"Lord, how can I be thankful and we didn't get the loan for our new home?"

"God, how can I be thankful when I didn't get promoted, knowing I work harder than the person who received the promotion?"

"Jesus, how can I be thankful and I don't have money for the necessities?"

"Father, how can I be thankful and we continue losing the baby we so desperately desire?"

Sometimes, it can seem difficult to *give thanks* in everything. And, how do we really give thanks in everything when life's circumstances scream and shout, "Put the covers back over your head and wait for tomorrow!"?

It is God's will that we give thanks in everything. He desires we remain thankful no matter what we encounter or experience. When we give thanks in everything: the promotion, the demotion, the setback, the breakthrough, in need, and/or in abundance, we prove we trust God's plans concerning our lives. We don't always see what God is doing, but we can always trust that He is working everything together for our good.

"Lord, thank you the loan was denied. I know that you have 'gone to prepare a place for me,' and the home you've prepared for me was not built by man" (John 14:2).

"God, thank you that I did not receive the promotion, because I know in 'due season I will reap if I do not lose heart'" (Galatians 6:9).

"Jesus, thank you for the season of no money in the bank because I learned that you are the supplier of every need, 'according to [Your] riches and glory'" (Philippians 4:19).

"Father, thank you for the loss I've experienced because it taught me how to 'lean not to my own understanding'" (Proverbs 3:5).

In everything, choose to give thanks—it is His will.

In Application

When has it been difficult to give thanks? Name at least three-five experiences or situations and find scriptures relating to your experiences that empower you to thank God.

Prayer

Father, I don't always understand life's circumstances and situations, but your word tells me to give thanks in all things, so today I am choosing to exhibit thankfulness. Lord, thank you for every moment I've tarried, thank you for every time you said, 'Not right now.' Thank you for everything because I know that it is your will for me. And, because it's your will, I need you to continue to strengthen my heart, so that I am reminded to give thanks no matter what I encounter. I love you Lord and I trust your will. I'll remain thankful. In Jesus' name, Amen.

The –Ing Family

Your journey of reaching your intended place will require perseverance and your commitment to seeing your vision through until fruition. However, you'll also need a bit of help from the –Ing Family. The –Ing Family is special, and very similar to our earthly families, the –Ing Family is with you no matter what. They will encourage you to continue your journey by reminding you to remain thankful, pushing you to rest, celebrate, give, pray, and fast. You will need the –Ing Family because they express the continuous actions you will need to take as you sprout to your intended place. The –Ing Family will be your roots and your lifeline, keeping you grounded, but giving you the nourishment you need to grow.

Double Vanities: Thanking

Today's Truth: "And this same God who takes care of me will supply all your needs from His glorious riches, which have been given to us in Christ Jesus." ~Philippians 4:19 NLT

Double Vanities: Thanking

Before moving into our house, we lived in a single bedroom apartment with one restroom, and it was just enough space for the two of us. When we decided to move, we knew there were a few upgraded features we wanted and needed, one of those being a master bathroom with double vanities. Thankfully, we found what we were looking for in a master.

Getting ready one morning, I stood in our master bathroom at the sink closest to the door. My husband came in, grabbed his toothbrush and the toothpaste, and headed for the door.

"Where are you going?" I questioned.

Looking confused, he turned and said, "In the other bathroom to brush my teeth."

"Why would you go in there—we have two sinks in here."

"You're right!"

I share that story because sometimes we ask God for something, to meet a need, give us more space, money, or even greater responsibility. However, when we get the "thing" we've asked for, we often neglect it or forget where He's brought us from. In our one bedroom, one bathroom apartment, we asked God to give us more space, but once He did, we were treating our new space like our old space.

As you sprout up, don't neglect to thank God for it all. Thank Him by using the tools He's given you, being mindful and appreciative of where He's brought you from and by celebrating your victories.

Sometimes we can become so familiar with a place or season in our lives we miss the opportunities to thank God.

In Application

What things have remained and what things have changed in your life? Create a list and thank God for each one of them for the next seven days.

God will supply, has supplied and is supplying all of your needs according to His riches in glory—thank Him.

Prayer

> *Heavenly Father, thank you for (insert the list of items you generated). Help my heart to always exude thankfulness, in Jesus' name, Amen.*

Praise the Lord: Celebrating

Today's Truth: "Praise the Lord. Praise God in His sanctuary; praise Him in His mighty heavens. Praise Him for His acts of power; praise Him for His surpassing greatness. Praise Him with the sounding of the trumpet, praise Him with the harp and the lyre, praise Him with the tambourine and dancing, praise Him with the strings and flute, praise Him with the clash of cymbals, praise Him with resounding cymbals. Let everything that has breath praise the Lord. Praise the Lord."
~Psalm 150 NIV

Praise the Lord: Celebrating

Most of the time we think of celebrations as parties "after" the big game, a family gathering "after" graduation, or the much needed vacation "after" all the hours worked, and indeed those are moments and times we should celebrate. But, who said celebrating should only be reserved for "after?"

Sprouting up takes hard work. It will require more of your time, energy, patience, and planned thought than anything you've decided to do before. Some of those days won't feel so great when you compare them to successes you've experienced in the past or measure them next to the future God has promised. However, David teaches in Psalm 34:1, "I will extol the Lord at all times; His praise will always be on my lips." Meaning, we should always celebrate God's work in our lives.

Celebrate along the way. You don't have to throw a party for every milestone, but you should keep track of those moments because with them you'll be able to look back and thank God. I've found comfort and excitement in seeing what God has already done because it assures me He will get me to the expected end He promised.

I'm not talking about false or exaggerated victories, but the times when you're facing lack and God provides miraculously. Or the time He sends a confirming word to the promise He made, or even when it feels like everything around you is sinking but you feel His peace—celebrate. Those moments are important to remember. Yes, where you are going is important. It matters, but it's not the only thing God has done for you.

Celebrate along the way. You'll be grateful you kept record of all the things God did for you.

In Application

Use the Celebration Chart to record the moments you see God move in your favor, even if it's not the anticipated end you have in mind. Pay attention this week to what God is doing for you, and find a reason to celebrate.

Prayer

Heavenly Father, I praise you for your acts of power; I praise you for your surpassing greatness. With everything I have, I praise you and your praise will continuously be on my lips all the days of my life. Thank you for fulfilling every promise and taking care of me along the way, in Jesus' name, Amen.

Celebration Chart

Pay attention to the details. God is always at work in your life. Record the breakthroughs and miracles you experience and witness in your life as you sprout up. Having these moments will add to your gratefulness, seeing what God has done and where He has made ways. Celebrate your journey.

January	February	March
April	**May**	**June**
July	**August**	**September**
October	**November**	**December**

Different Kinds: Resting

Today's Truth: "Do not be anxious about anything, but in everything, by prayer and petition, with thanksgiving, present your requests to God. And the peace of God, which transcends all understanding, will guard your hearts and your minds in Christ Jesus." ~Philippians 4:6-7 NIV

Different Kinds: Resting

It's often harder to receive help than it is to give it. We don't want to appear in need, in lack, or that we don't have the answers figured out. I didn't decide to leave my job without careful prayer and consideration. To some, it may have appeared my decision was thoughtless and emotional. It was indeed the opposite. It was exactly what God told me to do. Yet, I found it hard to rest.

Oftentimes, you pray and ask God for an answer, but when He gives the answer, it doesn't look the way you want, it's not what you expected, or how you believed He'd answer. It makes it difficult to rest because you wouldn't have handled "you" that way.

I'd been praying for God to get me to my intended place, and when He answered—I screamed, "THIS DOESN'T MAKE SENSE! I don't quit! I have a family to help support! What!"

And, I kept saying, "Lord, this can't be you, please give me the answer. I know you've given me this vision. Show me what to do Lord." All the while, it got harder and harder to remain and even harder to rest.

Finally, I broke. Deciding to leave was hard because it wasn't the answer I expected from God. How could I rest with a decision that left so much uncertainty? Leaving with another job secured, that makes sense, but leaving and there's nothing tangible—that seemed crazy.

I had to ask for help. My husband and I rearranged bill payments and made adjustments to our spending habits, and still I found it hard to rest.

I was depending on my abilities. I usually have things planned. I have things together, and it felt like every corner I turned there was a resounding "No." But God was teaching me something different. He was teaching me to be anxious for nothing—rest in me. He was teaching me through prayer and supplication (humble pleading) to make my requests known to Him—rest in me.

Did it always make sense? No!

It's hard to obey God's instruction to rest when the need stands firmly before you.

But, God supplied.

As you sprout, it's important to find rest in Christ. I'm sure when God reached the sixth day there was more He wanted to do, but He still rested. As Jesus walked the streets of Nazareth, there were always people to help, heal and deliver, but He obeyed His Father's command to rest.

God wants you to rest in the promise He's made you.

Rest on your journey. Resting shows God you trust Him to supply every need.

Rest! Close your eyes, think on God's goodness, worship Him, praise Him, and don't worry about the next step to take or how you will take care of this or that, God's got it. Receive His rest.

In Application

Be vulnerable with yourself and name what has you restless. Give it to God in prayer today and trust Him by doing what He has asked you to do even if it doesn't make sense.

Prayer

> *Heavenly Father, I have been so worried about (insert personal situation). I'm worried about (insert personal situation) because it makes me feel weak, but I know your word promises that when I am weak you are at perfect strength. Lord, I am also worried because I don't see how everything will work out and I have needs standing firmly before me. I know you do not want me to be anxious for anything, rather you tell me to make my requests known to you through prayer. I'm requesting your rest to overtake me, your peace to comfort my heart and mind and your hand to support, supply, and exceed every need I have or will have in the future, in Jesus' name, Amen.*

Give like Jesus: Giving

Today's Truth: "Be careful not to do your 'acts of righteousness' before men, to be seen by them. If you do, you will have no reward from your Father in Heaven. So when you give to the needy, do not announce it with trumpets, as the hypocrites do in the synagogues and on the streets, to be honored by men. I tell you the truth, they have received their reward in full. But when you give to the needy, do not let your left hand know what your right hand is doing, so that your giving may be in secret. Then your Father, who sees what is done in secret, will reward you." ~Matthew 6:1-4 NIV

Give Like Jesus

Turning left off the freeway, I was thinking about some of the things we needed to take care of that week. Honestly, it was more like the car was moving in the direction of home, but my mind was somewhere else.

Standing there at the exit, his sign read, "Homeless: will work for food." I didn't stop. I really didn't think any more about it.

Passing the gentleman, still thinking of my own need, I was stopped by the upcoming red light. Immediately a sense of responsibility came over me. I felt responsible for providing food to the gentleman holding the sign. I didn't know him and he didn't know me, yet it was in my heart to give.

How do you give when you feel you're in need?

How do you look past what you're facing to see someone else?

There are so many times I've needed something from God. Lord, I need you to deliver me from jealousy, anger, or a financial burden.

Jesus, with all power, could easily broadcast my needs and what He's done for me to the world. Rather, He chooses to meet our needs without announcing it with trumpets in the synagogues and on street corners to be honored by men. Jesus gives and gave in secret. He didn't yell from the cross, "Father, I didn't sin. I didn't cheat or lie. It was (insert your name)." He carried the cross, allowed the crowd to mock Him and the soldiers to beat Him. In an open display, He privately gave salvation. Give like Jesus.

The gentleman didn't need me to stop traffic or get out of my car for everyone to see me give him food. He didn't need to know my name or tell me what series of events led to his current situation.

As you're sprouting to the place God has for you, you will experience need, but you'll find that your sprout will also allow you to meet needs.

That day, I was pushed to let go of what I needed and see the need of someone else. Did my needs miraculously vanish? No. But, it strengthened my faith to believe if God cared for that man, and sent me to meet his need, He would send supply for my needs too. And He showed me that when it's within my power to act, I should (Proverbs 3:27).

I'm grateful Jesus doesn't stand on an open street corner pronouncing everything He's given me. I'm thankful He's not sharing every time He's fed me, clothed me, or delivered me from sin. Without a crowd or wanting applause, give like Jesus. What you do in secret, God will reward.

In Application

No matter what you need today, find a way to give. Sowing from your need will shift your perspective. Your private act(s) will be rewarded by our Father.

Prayer

> *Father, I stand in need of _____ today. Only you can meet my need, so I ask that you give to me again. I also ask that you present me with opportunities to give. In giving, my faith is strengthened, my belief renewed and my self-view is shifted to others. I'll give like you. Blow my mind, in Jesus' name, Amen.*

Be Strategic: Praying

Today's Truth: "But when you pray, go into your room, close the door and pray to your Father, who is unseen." ~ Matthew 6:6b NIV

Be Strategic: Praying

Ever heard the saying, "God likes to hear His word"? While I believe the saying is true (because it shows you've hidden His teachings in your heart), I really believe when we pray God's word, we are speaking life over ourselves and our situations.

As you embark upon this new journey, restart this chapter in your life, or even continue with the vision God has given you, prayer will be your lifeline.

Yes, God hears what we ask for in His son's name. However, a lot of times our asking is not speaking life. I could pray, "God please grow my business," and He hears me. Or I could pray Abraham's servant Laban's prayer, "Lord, I have started a business, 'please grant me success in the journey on which I have come'" (Genesis 24:42). This prayer is powerful because Abraham spoke "The Lord, before whom I have walked, will send His angel with you and make your journey a success." Because Abraham spoke the word of the Lord, Laban used the same language in faith, and he returned with Rebekah, who married Abraham's son Isaac. There's power in speaking God's word over your life and situation.

Be strategic when praying. Use God's word as a tool and watch things shift for you. God's word is life, and speaking His word breathes life over the things you've asked of Him.

In Application

Review the Powerful Prayers sheet. By continuously speaking God's word over your life, you will witness your sprout spurt. Start speaking God's word today!

Prayer

> *"Our Father in heaven, hallowed be your name, your kingdom come, your will be done on earth as it is in heaven. Give us today our daily bread. Forgive us our debts, as we also have forgiven our debtors. And lead us not into temptation, but deliver us from the evil one," in Jesus' name, Amen (Matthew 6:9-15 NIV).*

Powerful Prayers

The prayers below are prayers found in the word of God. Use Powerful Prayers when speaking to God. By using His word you are speaking life over yourself and your situation. Watch God unleash your future and move on your behalf as you use the word of God to pray.

Powerful Prayers

Laban's Prayer for Success	"O Lord, God of my master Abraham, if you will, please grant me success to the journey on which I have come." ~Genesis 24:42
Samson's Prayer for Strength	"O Sovereign Lord, remember me. O God, please strengthen me just once more." ~Judges 16:28
Hannah's Prayer of Adoration	"My heart rejoices in the Lord; in the Lord my horn is lifted high. My mouth boasts over my enemies, for I delight in your deliverance. There is no one holy like the Lord; there is no one besides you; there is no Rock like our God."~1 Samuel 2:1-2
Solomon's Prayer for Wisdom	"Give me your servant a discerning heart to govern your people and to distinguish between right and wrong. For who is able to govern this great people of yours?" ~1 Kings 3:9
Prayer of Jabez for Responsibility and Influence	"Bless me and enlarge my territory! Let your hand be with me, and keep me from harm so that I will be free from pain."~1Chronicles 4:10

King Asa's Prayer for God's protection	"Lord there is no one like you to help the powerless against the mighty. Help us, O Lord our God, for we rely on you, and in your name we have come against this vast army. O Lord, you are our God; do not let man prevail against you."~2 Chronicles 14:11
Nehemiah's Prayer of Forgiveness, Redemption, Success	"Lord, the God of heaven, the great and awesome God, who keeps His covenant of love with those who love Him and keep His commandments, let your ear be attentive and your eyes open to hear the prayer your servant is praying before you day and night for your servants, the people of Israel. I confess the sins we Israelites, including myself and my father's house, have committed against you. We have acted very wickedly toward you. We have not obeyed the commands, decrees and laws you gave your servant Moses.

Remember the instruction you gave your servant Moses, saying, 'If you are unfaithful, I will scatter you among the nations, but if you return to me and obey my commands, then even if your exiled people are at the farthest horizon, I will gather them from there and bring them to the place I have chosen as a dwelling for my Name.'

They are your servants and your people, whom you redeemed by your great strength and your mighty hand. Lord, let your ear be attentive to the prayer of this your servant |

	and to the prayer of your servants who delight in revering your name. Give your servant success today by granting him favor in the presence of this man." ~Nehemiah 1:4-11
David's Prayer on Trust	"To you, O Lord, I lift up my soul; in you I trust, O my God. Do not let me be put to shame, nor let my enemies triumph over me. No one whose hope is in you will ever be put to shame, but they will be put to shame who are treacherous without excuse. Show me your ways, O Lord, teach me your paths; guide me in your truth and teach me, for you are God my Savior." ~Psalm 25: 1-5
Jeremiah's Prayer for God's help	"Although our sins testify against us, O Lord, do something for the sake of your name." ~Jeremiah 14:7
King Nebuchadnezzar's Prayer for God's strength and power	"How great are His signs, how mighty His wonders! His kingdom is an eternal kingdom; His dominion endures from generation to generation." ~Daniel 4:3
Jonah's Prayer of bringing Life to dead situations	"In my distress I called to the Lord, and He answered me. From the depths of the grave I called for help and you listened to my cry. You hurled me into the deep, into the very heart of the seas, and His currents swirled about me; all your waves and breakers swept over me. I said, 'I have been banished from your sight; yet I will look again toward your holy temple.' The engulfing waters threatened me, the deep surrounded me; seaweed was wrapped around my head. To the roots

	of the mountains I sank down; the earth beneath barred me in forever. But you brought my life up from the pit, O Lord my God. 'When my life was ebbing away, I remembered you, Lord, and my prayer rose to you, to your holy temple. Those who cling to worthless idols forfeit the grace that could be theirs. But I, with a song of thanksgiving, will sacrifice to you. What I have voiced I will make good. Salvation comes from the Lord." ~Jonah 2:1-9
Habakkuk's Prayer for Vision	"Lord, I have heard of your fame; I stand in awe of your deed, O Lord. Renew them in our day, in our time make them known; in wrath remember mercy." ~Habakkuk 3:2
Mary's Prayer for Blessings	"My soul glorifies the Lord and my spirit rejoices in God my Savior, for He has been mindful of the humble state of His servant. From now on all generations will call me blessed, for the Mighty One has done great things for me—holy is His name." ~Luke 1:46-49
Jesus' Prayer for God's will	"Father, if you are willing, take this cup from me; yet not my will, but your will be done." ~Luke 22:42

It's More than Important: Fasting

Today's Truth: "When you fast, do not look somber as the hypocrites do, for they disfigure their faces to show men they are fasting. I tell you the truth, they have received their reward in full. But when you fast, put oil on your head, wash your face, so that it will not be obvious to men that you are fasting, but only to your Father, who is unseen; and your Father, who sees what is done in secret, will reward you."
~Matthew 6:16-18 NIV

It's More than Important: Fasting

Sprouting disrupts your normal flow and pattern. It may mean you are putting in more hours on a project, having to study in order to gain more knowledge, or even work a bit harder to either obtain or refine a skill. Being pulled in all those directions gets noisy, and it may feel like you are constantly thinking and working.

Fasting quiets your flesh. It silences the noise so you're able to hear God's voice clearly and without question.

I remember the very first time I fasted; I fasted for seven days because I needed direction from God. I was in a place in my life where I felt I didn't know what to do or how to handle things that were occurring— it was extremely noisy. As I fasted, God began to provide clear direction, strengthened my belief in Him, and gave me supernatural power to control my flesh.

Getting to your intended place will require your labor, but it will also require hearing God clearly.

Fasting refreshes your spirit, as does any encounter with God. When fasting, your flesh is put under subjection and your relationship with God is made stronger. Fasting is and will be an integral component to sprouting up, as it begins to open the door to God's promises.

Fasting builds your position on discipline because it's a private sacrifice that often brings public reward. When you fast, your sprout bursts through the ground with clear direction and purpose. Don't allow your flesh to control or delay what God wants to do today.

Take a note from Jesus in Matthew 3:16-4:11—fast. Fast and watch the windows of Heaven open and pour you out blessings you do not have room to receive.

On this journey, be dedicated to keeping your flesh under subjection through giving, prayer, and fasting and watch God accelerate your ministry and all those things connected to you.

In Application

Pray and ask God to show when and how to conduct your fast. Remember, there is no convenient time to fast, but it's always convenient to receive His blessings. Choose to give up a meal, choose to give up social media—choose to give up something. God will reward your discipline.

Prayer

Heavenly Father, at the end of the day, it was the lack of discipline to say no to food that changed the fellowship you desired to have with us. Thank you for sending your son Jesus not only to die on the cross for our sins, but also for living a disciplined life before us. Jesus was disciplined in giving His time, resources, energy, and love. He was disciplined in spending time with you in prayer, to understand your plan and your ways, and He disciplined His flesh through fasting. Give me the strength to fast, so that our relationship is made stronger and I may hear you more clearly, in Jesus' name, Amen.

As you grow...

You will experience days when the light isn't beaming from the end of a tunnel. Rather, it feels the light is so small you're squinting to see or feel it on your face.

I believe David said it best in 2 Samuel 24:24, "No, I insist on paying you for it. I will not sacrifice to the Lord my God burnt offerings that cost me nothing." Your sprout will cost you something. Fulfilling the vision God has for your life won't come without a price. But, would you really want to give God something that didn't cost you anything? It has been my experience that when I pay for something there is more value there. I often take better care of the item(s) or place more importance on it/them. My stories, the devotionals, and experiences I share have cost me something...and I don't necessarily mean monetarily. For Paul to share the gospel, it cost him—the thorn in his side.

Prepare your heart and mind to pay your price, and ask God to heighten your awareness to the tricks and schemes of Satan, as not to fall. His tricks generally disguise themselves as death, an argument between you and your spouse, family or closest friend, the feeling to quit, getting side-tracked, confusion—you see where I'm going. God does not intend for your wait to become weight; be anxious for nothing along on this journey. Don't stop working and stay alert. God is shifting the ground beneath you. Prepare for your harvest!

Sprouting is great, but be prepared for the adversity.

Remain faithful to God and the purpose He's placed in your heart. It's your time, and the seasons of your life have definitely yielded the perfect conditions to bring forth your purpose.

Sprout now! Sprout up!

I pray you were encouraged, challenged and inspired to live God's truth for your life, in Jesus' name, Amen.

ABOUT THE AUTHOR

Jossalyn Richardson Wilson

Passionate and eager to share God's word with the world, Jossalyn is a sought after speaker, mentor, and coach. She is dedicated to encourage, inspire, and challenge today's generation to identify their kingdom purpose and live God's truth for their life.

A native of Spartanburg, South Carolina, Jossalyn attended the University of South Carolina, Columbia. Graduating with a degree in English, Jossalyn joined Teach For America and spent three years in the classroom leading students to their fullest potential. After teaching, Jossalyn transitioned to Teach For America staff as a manager, coaching, developing, and equipping teachers with best practices, data analysis skills and proven resources. Currently, Jossalyn is completing her professional Coaching Certificate with Queens University in Charlotte, North Carolina.

In 2012, Jossalyn became the founder and CEO of Jossalyn's Journey, a consulting firm equipping and empowering teenage girls (ages 13-

17) to explore their life's purpose and build lasting skills to excel in today's society. She also publishes an online devotional, Jotting Truth, which empowers and encourages people to seek hard, far and wide after God.

Proudly her heart beats as a wife to Darryl, mother to Luke, daughter, sister, and friend. Jossalyn is the new author of the 21 day devotional, *Sprout Up: 21 Days of Getting to Your Intended Place.*

To book Jossalyn for your next event, workshop, conference or seminar, visit: http://www.jottingtruth.com/contact/.

Jossalyn's Journey (JJ) is a consulting firm that coaches, encourages, and equips teenage ladies (ages 13-17) with the skills to live intentionally and excel in today's society. Through Jossalyn's Journey, Sunflowers explore their life's purpose, celebrate and refine their journey, and learn how to invest in others.

Jossalyn's Journey is designed to connect relationally with each Sunflower, helping them develop the skills and tools they need to shine and positively stand out in our noisy world. An annual conference is held to bring all Sunflowers together in order to share experiences, strengthen relationships, learn, and grow together.

Subscribe to Jossalyn's Journey to receive emails and Parent Petals with tips and information on parent to daughter relationships.

Get Involved with Jossalyn's Journey
Visit: www.jossalynsjourney.com to obtain more information.
Email: info@jossalynsjourney.com

Jossalyn Richardson Wilson writes an online devotional, Jotting Truth. Jotting Truth challenges, encourages, and inspires you to live God's truth. The devotional is published every Monday, Wednesday, and Friday. Subscribe to Jotting Truth to receive your FREE download.

Jotting Truth also celebrates those who are living their purpose—living truth. If you or someone you know is living the purpose God has for you, use the Living Truth link to share your truth. You could be featured on Jotting Truth.

Get encouragement throughout your week, subscribe to Jotting Truth today.

Visit: www.jottingtruth.com
Living Truth: http://www.jottingtruth.com/living-truth/

Thank you for reading this book. If you enjoyed it, please leave a review at your favorite retailer's website.

To order additional copies of Sprout Up! please visit:
https://squareup.com/market/jotting-truth

For bulk ordering please email:
books@jossalynsjourney.com

www.ingramcontent.com/pod-product-compliance
Lightning Source LLC
Chambersburg PA
CBHW072102290426
44110CB00014B/1788